D1491811

How Things Work

Interactive Quiz

Managing Editors: Simon Melhuish and Sarah Wells

Series Editor: Nikole G Bamford

Designer: Linley J Clode

Writers: Nick Daws, Anne Vasey

Cover Design: Radio

Published by
The Lagoon Group
PO Box 311, KT2 5QW, UK
PO Box 990676, Boston, MA 02199, USA

ISBN: 1904797598

www.intelliquestbooks.com

Printed in China

IntelliQuest

UNIQUE BOOK CODE	031

Instructions

First of all make sure you
have a Quizmo –

Find the book's unique code (this
appears at the top of this page).
Use the < and > buttons to scroll
to this number on the Quizmo screen.
Press the ⏎ button to enter the
code, and you're ready to go.

Use the < > scroll buttons to select
the question number you want to
answer. Press the A, B, C, or D
button to enter your chosen answer.

If you are correct the green light beside
the button you pressed will flash. You can then
use the scroll button to move on to another question.

If your answer is incorrect, the red light beside the
button you pressed will flash.

Don't worry, you can try again and again until you have the correct answer, OR move on to another question. (Beware: the more times you guess incorrectly, the lower your final percentage score will be!)

You can finish the quiz at any point – just press the ⬌ button to find out your score and rank as follows:

75% or above	You're a genius! You can make anything work.
50% – 74%	The workings of your mind are obviously quite advanced!
25% – 49%	Keep that brain working at it!
Less than 25%	You're a few cogs short of a machine!

If you do press the ⬌ button to find out your score, this will end your session and you will have to use the ⬌ to start again!

HAVE FUN!

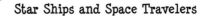

You need to know masses about the science and technology of space travel and exploration to become an astronaut. The cosmos is just outside your window so here are a few questions to start you off and even if you don't want to be a space traveler yourself, the science behind it is mindblowing.

001

How fast must a rocket fly in order to escape Earth's gravity completely and travel into outer space - otherwise known as escape velocity?

A) 1,052mph/1,694kph
B) 15,404mph/24,800kph
C) 25,039mph/40,313kph
D) 105,658mph/170,109kph

002

How many main engines does the orbiter section of a Space Shuttle have?

A) 1
B) 3
C) 0
D) 2

Why do astronauts sometimes report the sensation that they are flying upside-down?

- **A)** In weightless conditions, the astronauts float away from their seats and may bump their heads on the roof of the spacecraft
- **B)** There is no fixed horizon in the view from the window, and this causes astronauts to become disorientated
- **C)** In the microgravity conditions of space, the astronauts' blood is still pumping as it would on Earth, where it must resist gravity
- **D)** The spacecraft rotates and turns in flight, with the floor and the roof trading places

Why do rockets usually turn eastwards after launch?

- **A)** The Earth rotates to the east, so the rocket benefits from a natural boost
- **B)** The Earth rotates to the west, so the rocket benefits from a natural boost
- **C)** To avoid the sun shining into the astronauts' eyes
- **D)** To head towards the Pacific for splashdown

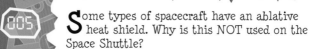

005

Some types of spacecraft have an ablative heat shield. Why is this NOT used on the Space Shuttle?

A) The astronauts get very cold in outer space and look forward to getting warm on re-entry to the atmosphere

B) The tiles are very heavy

C) The tiles don't fit the curvature of the shuttle's fuselage

D) The Shuttle is meant to be re-usable, but ablative shields burn off and can only be used once

006

Why are the cargo bay doors of a space shuttle opened shortly after it goes into orbit?

A) To cool the orbiter

B) As part of a test routine for all parts of the shuttle

C) To allow the astronauts to inspect the shuttle for any damage during launch

D) To jettison unwanted cargo

Which of these is NOT a reason for siting the Hubble Telescope in outer space?

A) Water vapor in the atmosphere can blur the image

B) Air currents in the Earth's atmosphere can distort light

C) Dust in the atmosphere can cause a fuzzy image

D) The distance to the stars and planets being observed is shorter, so the image is clearer

---

Which of these statements about the orbital velocity of a satellite is FALSE?

A) A satellite must travel fast enough to resist the Earth's gravity, but not so fast that it flies off into space

B) The nearer to Earth a satellite orbits, the slower its velocity needs to be

C) A satellite in geostationary orbit is traveling at a velocity and altitude such that it stays over one point on the Earth's surface

D) The moon is a satellite that has an orbital velocity of about 2,300mph

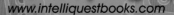

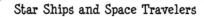
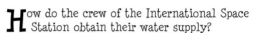
009

How do the crew of the International Space Station obtain their water supply?

A) It is recycled, for example by condensing the vapor in the crew's breath

B) It is all supplied in large tanks brought from Earth at regular intervals

C) No water is used - the crew do not take a bath, and they drink cans of fizzy pop

D) It is manufactured by burning hydrogen in the presence of oxygen

010

How does the Mission Control Center in Houston, Texas, make astronauts aware that it's time to wake up from their sleep while they are traveling in space?

A) They yell out, "Wakey, wakey! Rise and shine!"

B) They raise the blinds on the windows, allowing the sunlight to flood into the cabin

C) They sound an alarm bell

D) They play a favorite song or piece of music chosen by one of the crew members

What does a satellite in polar orbit do?

A) It remains stationary over the North or South Pole

B) It has a very small orbit, centered around the North or South Pole

C) It becomes extremely cold

D) It passes once over each of the Poles of the Earth during each orbit

---

How is a Simplified Aid for Extravehicular Activity Rescue (SAFER) unit used during spacewalking?

A) It's a backpack unit worn by astronauts, in case they become separated from the spacecraft. It uses a nitrogen gas-propelled rocket maneuvering system

B) It's an extendable framework which astronauts on board the spacecraft can use to rescue a colleague in distress

C) It's an extra-strong polyester fiber rope that the astronaut uses to attach himself securely to the spacecraft

D) It's a stun gun to immobilize any aliens who attack the astronauts

013

Why are space suits usually white?

A) To reflect sunlight and control temperature inside the suit

B) For hygiene reasons, so any contamination can be quickly removed

C) To make the astronaut highly visible during spacewalks

D) It was the designer's favorite color

014

How did exploring the Moon help medicine on Earth?

A) People who took an interest in the progress of the missions were found to be healthier than those who didn't

B) Measuring the functions of the human body on the Moon helped doctors to understand better how it works on Earth

C) Compounds of substances found on the Moon were found to have medical uses

D) Digital image processing was developed to allow computer enhancement of Moon pictures. This technology is now used in hospital equipment such as MRI and CAT scan machines

Star Ships and Space Travelers

Why is a space suit inflated like a balloon?

015

- **A)** To protect the astronaut from vibration and knocks during space travel
- **B)** To provide a pressurized environment, as the lack of atmospheric pressure in space would cause the astronaut's blood to boil
- **C)** To reduce the effects of weightlessness on the astronaut's body
- **D)** Releasing a valve in the suit allows astronauts to propel themselves around in weightless conditions

What is normally delivered to the crew of the International Space Station around every six months?

016

- **A)** Supplies of chocolate and candy bars
- **B)** A new Soyuz capsule that will act as their return vehicle, or as a lifeboat in the event of an emergency
- **C)** Tanks of fresh air to replenish the atmosphere
- **D)** Clean laundry

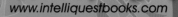

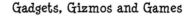

Just what is it about gadgets, gizmos and games that is amazingly intriguing. The question that arises so often is - just how do they do that? In the following questions you get to find out how a few of them do operate and if you know the answers already then you must be mad about gadgets.

What makes a light stick glow?

A) The stick is a magic wand, and snapping it triggers a spell to make it glow

B) The stick is filled with naturally occurring phosphorescent substances extracted from seawater. Inside is a vial of sodium chloride, which causes them to glow when broken

C) The stick is filled with crystals. Snapping the stick introduces heat and energy that melts the crystals, so they become glowing liquid

D) The stick is filled with a substance called phenyl oxalate ester and fluorescent dye. Inside is a glass vial of hydrogen peroxide. Snapping the stick breaks the vial, mixing the chemicals, which react and glow

What is Trilateration?

A) The way that an altimeter calculates your distance above sea level

B) Walking sideways to keep your balance when descending a steep slope

C) The process by which a GPS receiver mathematically calculates your position by measuring your distance from satellites orbiting the Earth

D) The direction of the Earth's magnetic field, which turns the needle of a compass

How does a thermal imaging camera let you see in the dark?

A) It uses a special film that is sensitive to infrared radiation rather than visible light

B) It contains infrared detectors, which pick up infrared waves (heat) being emitted by the objects in view, producing a thermogram

C) It focuses an infrared beam on the objects in view and monitors the level at which they reflect it back

D) It warms up your eyes, making them more sensitive

www.intelliquestbooks.com

020

What fuel is used in a modern Olympic torch?

A) A sacred gas from Mount Olympus in Greece

B) A mixture of gases such as propane and butane, stored under pressure in liquid form

C) An aluminum canister of gaseous methane

D) A cotton wick soaked in refined petroleum

021

What is GPS?

A) Global Positioning System: a small receiver device which tells you your location anywhere on the Earth's surface

B) Goal Positioning System: a sophisticated type of electronic compass that tells you the direction and distance of your destination

C) Great Pair of Socks: specially cushioned for hikers' feet

D) Grand Polar Statistics: a device that gives your distance from the poles and equator of the Earth and sea level

How does a pinball machine know that you have tried to cheat by tilting the machine?

022

A) There is a system of ball bearings inside the base. If they roll too far out of line, it sets off the alarm

B) Inside there is a pendulum bob hanging in a metal ring. If the pendulum touches the ring, the machine has been tilted too much

C) A tiny pinball wizard sits inside the machine. If he falls off his chair, you have tilted it too far

D) Sensors on all sides of the machine are linked to its computer

Why do some 3-D glasses have one red lens and one green lens?

023

A) No reason - it's just to make everyone laugh

B) Red represents the action closest to you, and green is further away

C) 3-D only works in black and white, so the glasses filter out the color

D) Two slightly different images are displayed on the movie screen, one in red and the other in green. Each of your eyes sees a different image through the filters, and your brain joins them together

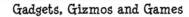

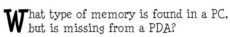

024

What type of memory is found in a PC, but is missing from a PDA?

    A) RAM

    B) ROM

    C) The hard drive

    D) Brain cells

025

How are the vibrations of an electric guitar's strings normally amplified?

    A) The strings are electrified, and this allows them to make an audible vibration by themselves

    B) As in an acoustic guitar, the hollow body and soundboard develop the string vibrations, which are then transmitted electronically to the amp and speaker

    C) The end of each string is attached to a wire that connects to the amp and speaker

    D) A magnetic pick-up transmits an electronic signal to an amplifier and speaker

Gadgets, Gizmos and Games

How does a bowling pin-setter know which pins have fallen over?

A) A scanner camera is mounted further down the lane

B) There is a sensor underneath each pin

C) It uses a miniature radar system

D) An attendant in a booth keeps watch and enters the information into a computer

---

How does the touch-screen on a PDA record the pressure of the stylus?

A) Current is passed alternately between horizontal and vertical silver bars along the edges of the screen, making a voltage field. Pressing with the stylus disturbs the field

B) There is a tiny magnet in the point of the stylus, and sensors around the screen detect its position

C) Hundreds of tiny sensors are located under the screen. Pressing with the stylus makes contact with them

D) The stylus contains invisible ink

At the Movies

There are lots of movie buffs out there but do they know the technicalities of movie-making? If you don't already know why cinema is referred to as the silver screen or the basics of CGI then you will definitely find out here. Answer these questions and don't forget the popcorn.

028

Where is the best place to sit if you want to experience the sound system in a movie theater?

A) Halfway back from the screen, exactly in the middle

B) About two-thirds back from the screen, slightly off-center

C) Front row, dead center

D) In the projection room

029

Which of the following would NOT be used to create creature effects make-up?

A) Modeling clay

B) Salt

C) Poly vinyl chloride

D) Foam latex

Why do film-makers use blue screens to create different backgrounds?

A) Blue is a popular color among people in the film industry

B) A special camera is used, which is not sensitive to blue. It only records the action taking place in front of the screen, so a different background can then be added

C) Actors are filmed in front of the screen, and the blue area is then replaced by a different background that has been filmed separately

D) Blue is the color of the sea and the sky. An artist will later paint clouds or waves onto the film to create a realistic background

What happens if an actress wears a blue dress in a blue screen scene?

A) She will appear to be naked!

B) Her body will disappear!

C) The dress will appear three-dimensional, while the remainder of the scene remains flat

D) The dress will appear red

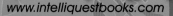

At the Movies

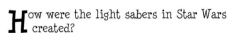

032

How were the light sabers in Star Wars created?

A) The actors used fluorescent light sticks, and the image was manually smudged on the film later to give the glowing effect

B) The actors were filmed using plain sticks, then a color animation of the light sabers was created and shot separately. The two films were combined

C) Genuine light sabers were used for authenticity

D) The actors fought empty-handed, and an image of the light saber was drawn onto the film with fluorescent ink

033

Why are movie screens covered in tiny perforations?

A) Air conditioning units behind the screen blow air through the theater

B) Theater staff can peep through to watch the audience unseen

C) There are speakers behind the screen, and this allows the sound to pass through

D) To reduce the weight of the screen

At the Movies

Which of these methods might an expert use to make a computer-generated dinosaur in a movie?

A) Travel back in time and photograph a real dinosaur in action

B) Create an animation using cartoon drawings of a dinosaur, then enhance it to look like photography

C) Make a clay model of the animal, then scan it into the computer using lasers

D) Generate a 3-D image using only 2-D artists' impressions

034

What is an optical-compositing machine used for?

A) To enhance the colors on a piece of film that looks drab

B) To synchronize the pictures with the sound in a movie, when they have been recorded separately

C) To enable short-sighted producers to see the film clearly

D) To precisely combine two separate pieces of film, giving the illusion that this is a single piece of footage

035

036

To make a realistic computer generated image of an ocean wave, what would you need to do?

A) Program the computer to understand the particle systems of the water and how its atoms interact with each other and other factors like gravity, wind etc

B) Film the real ocean extensively, and feed the images into the computer to analyze

C) Lay a network of sensors in the ocean and record the data in the computer

D) Film ripples in a bathtub, and then use the computer to enlarge them

037

Why is the world of movies sometimes called "the silver screen?"

A) In memory of the days of black-and-white movies, with their silver-grey colored pictures

B) Early movie screens were made from polished silver

C) It refers to the reflective coating that is added to the matte white vinyl of a movie screen

D) Movie stars earn a lot of silver dollars

What is the Z-Buffer in terms of creating 3-D graphics?

    A) It calculates the number of polygon shapes needed to form a realistic natural shape, such as a human body

    B) It creates correct perspective, assigning each object a number based on its position along an imaginary line, going from the screen back to the horizon

    C) It creates the variations of surface color and texture that make objects look real

    D) It's a cushion that catches the designers if they fall asleep while working on complex graphics

038

Which of these is NOT part of the mechanism of a Steadicam movie camera?

    A) Articulated arm with a spring, pulley and cable arrangement

    B) Special shoes with foam soles

    C) Supportive vest

    D) "Sled" that holds the camera, monitor and battery

039

040

Which of these statements about digital cinema is TRUE?

A) A digital recording will be much higher quality than a conventional 35mm film

B) Picture quality stays the same no matter how many times the movie is projected - it doesn't suffer from scratches and dust

C) Digital video is more expensive than conventional film

D) A DVD-ROM can't be used to record a copy of a digital movie

041

An IMAX movie screen can be as large as an eight-story apartment block - how do they project such a huge image?

A) A bank of 10 separate projectors is used to display different segments of the image

B) A special lens is placed in front of the projector, to enlarge the image

C) There is no projector - the screen is like an enormous TV screen

D) The film is 10 times bigger than standard 35 mm film, and a projector weighing about two tons is used

Flying Sky High

From time immemorial we have been obsessed with flying and soaring on the breezes like birds. Are you fascinated by flying too? Answer these questions and see how much you know about those marvelous men and their flying machines.

What are the four basic aerodynamic forces that work in opposing directions to keep an aircraft in flight?

A) Lift, thrust, weight and drag

B) Speed, height, distance and wind

C) North, south, east and west

D) Gravity, power, lift and altitude

Which of the following sounds does the "black box" flight recorder on an aircraft record?

A) Switches being thrown in the cockpit

B) Cockpit conversations

C) Cargo being loaded into the hold

D) Maintenance to an engine being carried out shortly before take-off

Flying Sky High

044

Why does an aircraft have wings whereas a spacecraft usually does not?

- **A)** The aircraft would pitch and roll, tipping passengers off their seats, without wings. Astronauts do not mind this as they are strapped in securely
- **B)** Lift is created by air passing around the wing. There is no air in space, so wings are not necessary
- **C)** The effect of gravity causes an aircraft to sink without wings. There is no gravity in space, so wings are not necessary
- **D)** Wings look more attractive, and are added because more people see an aircraft

---

045

Why does a helicopter have a small rotor blade on its tail?

- **A)** It controls the direction of motion
- **B)** It acts as a back-up if the main rotor should fail
- **C)** It keeps the tail from sinking towards the ground
- **D)** It counteracts the tendency of the body of the helicopter to spin when the main rotor blade is turning

What is the main way in which an air traffic controller can identify craft flying through his/her area?

   A) The controller looks through binoculars

   B) The controller makes radio contact with the pilot and requests his/her identity

   C) A transponder in the airplane produces a radio signal in response to incoming radar from the ground

   D) Details of the flight are emailed to each controller in the region where the aircraft will travel

Why does a glider have very long, thin wings?

   A) To reduce the amount of drag, making the wings more efficient

   B) To reduce the weight of the aircraft as much as possible

   C) It does not require wide wings, as they do not need to support an engine or propeller

   D) The long wings are needed to give the glider stability

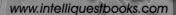

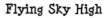

Flying Sky High

048

Where are "ailerons" found and what do they do?

A) They are small foils on the tail of the aircraft, used to adjust direction and altitude

B) They are the equivalent of a car's windshield wipers, used to maintain visibility from the cockpit

C) They are flaps on the outer ends of aircraft wings, used for turning and leveling the craft

D) They are ornamental flaps on the pilot's uniform, used to distinguish the captain from the co-pilot

049

Why does an aircraft retract its wheels after take-off?

A) To protect the tires from the freezing temperatures in the upper atmosphere, which would damage them

B) To give a more streamlined appearance

C) To protect the wheels from damage due to hitting objects such as birds

D) To reduce the surface area of the plane as it passes through the air, which in turn reduces drag

Flying Sky High

How does an aircraft wing create lift?

A) The sharp leading edge of the wing has so little resistance to the air that the aircraft becomes effectively almost weightless at high speed

B) The wing acts like a sail, and the air current is collected by it and used to push the aircraft upwards

C) The shape of the wing causes deflections of the air current, and this causes low air pressure above the wing but high pressure below it

D) The wing does not create lift - the engines of the aircraft raise it into the air

Where are the horizontal and vertical stabilizers on an aircraft?

A) They are flaps on the underside of the wings

B) They are sensors on either side of the cockpit

C) They are extendable sections on the tips of the wings

D) They are the wing-shaped horizontal and vertical pieces on the tail

050

051

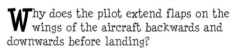

052

Why does the pilot extend flaps on the wings of the aircraft backwards and downwards before landing?

A) The flaps are to slow the aircraft down as it approaches the runway

B) The force of gravity increases as the aircraft comes closer to the ground, so a larger wing is needed to support it

C) At low speeds, the aircraft requires more lift than when cruising. The flaps alter the shape of the wing to provide this

D) The change in temperature from the upper to the lower atmosphere causes tension in the wing structure, and the movement of the flaps releases this

053

What does the cyclic control in a helicopter do?

A) It controls lateral direction (forwards/backwards/left/right)

B) It controls vertical direction (upwards and downwards)

C) It causes the helicopter to rotate

D) It allows the helicopter to hover in a stationary position

What is a Pitot tube?

054

A) A speaking tube in the cockpit that allows the pilot to give instructions to the crew

B) A sensor on the tail of an aircraft. It measures direction by pivoting as the aircraft turns

C) A sensor on the wing of an aircraft. It measures air speed by detecting the pressure of air entering a small tube

D) A sensor in the fuel tank of an aircraft. The fuel level in the small tube remains constant even when the aircraft pitches

How does a skydiver use a drogue chute?

055

A) It's a reserve canopy that can be released if the main chute fails

B) It's a small parachute that is released before the main canopy, pulling the main one out

C) It's a stunt chute allowing the skydiver to perform loops and turns

D) It's a small canopy that is opened to slow down the rate of free fall

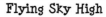

056

How is the air in a balloon re-heated during flight?

A) Cylinders of hydrogen are carried in the basket. A pilot light ignites the gas when it is switched on

B) Cylinders of compressed propane are carried in the basket and piped to the burner. A pilot light ignites the gas when it is switched on

C) A brazier of charcoal is kept lit. When an extra boost is needed, an air pump is switched on to increase the temperature

D) There is a tank of petrol underneath the burner. A switch generates a spark to ignite it when needed

057

At what speed must air pass over a hang glider to create lift?

A) No air current is required

B) About 5-6 mph/8-10 kph

C) About 40-60 mph/64-97 kph

D) About 15-25 mph/24-40 kph

What is the basic principle of physics behind hot air balloons?

- **A)** Hot air has more energy than cool air, because the molecules are moving faster
- **B)** Hot air contained within a sack will attempt to move towards the cooler air outside
- **C)** Hot air is lighter than cool air, because it has less mass per unit of volume
- **D)** A spherical object has a tendency to rise

Both a blimp and a balloon use gas to generate lift, but how do they differ?

- **A)** A blimp is not able to hover whereas a balloon can
- **B)** A balloon should not be used to display advertising whereas a blimp is often used for this
- **C)** A blimp can move forwards and maneuver under its own power whereas a balloon cannot
- **D)** A blimp uses helium at the outside temperature, but in a balloon the helium is heated

On a planet two-thirds covered by water we were bound to learn to navigate the waves. Just how do vessels travel for miles on and under the sea? See if you know by answering the following questions.

060

The Archimedes principle explains how ships can float even when they are made of substances such as steel that would normally sink in water. It states that a body immersed in a fluid is buoyed up by a force equal to:

A) The weight of the object concerned
B) The density of the displaced fluid
C) The Earth's gravitational pull
D) The weight of the displaced fluid

061

A submarine has ballast tanks that allow it to control its buoyancy. What are these tanks filled with when the submarine is on the surface of the sea?

A) Air
B) Water
C) Lead
D) Hydrogen

And what are the ballast tanks filled with when the submarine wishes to descend?

062

- **A)** Carbon dioxide
- **B)** Sand
- **C)** Air
- **D)** Water

Submarines may be powered by diesel engines or nuclear reactors. What is the big advantage of nuclear submarines compared with diesel?

063

- **A)** Cheaper to run
- **B)** They're bigger
- **C)** Can stay at sea and/or underwater much longer
- **D)** Cause less pollution

SCUBA stands for Self-Contained Underwater Breathing Apparatus. Which well-known ocean explorer is credited as its co-inventor?

064

- **A)** Captain Haddock
- **B)** Jacques Cousteau
- **C)** Jules Verne
- **D)** Captain Cook

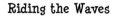

065

SCUBA divers breathe either compressed air or an oxygen-enriched gas called Nitrox. As well as the gas tank, another essential piece of equipment is the regulator. What does this do?

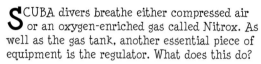

A) Ensures you don't run out of air by warning you when there is only a small amount left

B) Ensures you adhere to all the rules and regulations while you are diving

C) Slows down your breathing, to stop you using up your air supply too fast

D) Reduces the pressure from the tank to a safe level to inhale, and supplies air on-demand

066

If SCUBA divers return to the surface too quickly, they risk suffering from a painful and possibly fatal condition called "the bends." What is the cause of this condition?

A) Blood rushing away from the brain due to moving upwards

B) Excess oxygen causing blood vessels in the brain to swell

C) Bubbles of nitrogen gas forming in the diver's bloodstream

D) The sudden change in temperature as the diver returns to the surface

Riding the Waves

Which of these pieces of equipment is used to treat divers who have returned to the surface too quickly, perhaps due to an emergency?

    A) Compression chamber
    B) Torture chamber
    C) Combustion chamber
    D) Decompression chamber

What is one thing you should NEVER do in SCUBA gear?

    A) Monkey impressions
    B) Hold your breath
    C) Touch another diver
    D) Breathe steadily

What is the main method used by submarines for navigating underwater and locating targets?

    A) Radar
    B) Visual navigation
    C) Sonar
    D) Lasers

070 At low speeds hydrofoils sit on the sea like normal boats, but at high speed they rise out of the water, reducing drag and allowing the vessel to travel more efficiently. They rise due to:

A) A curtain of air forming under the vessel

B) Increased buoyancy from reducing the ballast

C) Lift produced by the underwater hydrofoils

D) A hard-working team of mermaids

071 Hovercraft can ride on a cushion of air over sea or land. Which of these statements about them is NOT true?

A) Unlike conventional boats, hovercraft do not create a wake on water

B) A hovercraft can pass over bird's eggs without breaking them

C) A hovercraft's engine should never be switched off over water, as it will sink

D) In an emergency, the quickest way to stop a hovercraft is to turn off its engine

We've come a long way since the age of steam. From snail's pace to hurtling speeds, upright to leaning, trains and trams are still carrying millions of passengers a day but do you know how? See how much of a train enthusiast you are and answer these questions to test your knowledge.

How do San Francisco's cable cars move?

072

A) They have electric motors in them
B) They are pulled along by an underground cable
C) They have diesel motors in them
D) They are pulled along by an overhead cable

How do San Francisco's cable cars differ from those on a funicular railway?

073

A) They have their own power source
B) They cannot operate on hills
C) They do not have brakes
D) They can stop and start independently

074

Funicular railways are often used on steep slopes which ordinary trains would be unable to negotiate. By what means are the cars on a funicular railway powered?

A) Electric motors
B) Diesel motors
C) Cable and a counterbalancing train
D) Nuclear reactors

075

High-speed maglev trains could provide the mass transportation system of the future. What does maglev stand for?

A) Magnetic lever
B) Magnetic levitation
C) Magnet leveler
D) Magical levitation

076

Walt Disney World's Monorail System near Orlando, Florida, has one of the highest riderships of all monorails. How many passenger trips are recorded each day?

A) Over 100,000
B) Over 80,000
C) Over 70,000
D) Over 60,000

Up to what speeds will maglev trains be able to run?

   A) Over 100 mph/161 kph
   B) Over 200 mph/322 kph
   C) Over 400 mph/644 kph
   D) Over 300 mph/483 kph

As well as having only one rail, what (according to The Monorail Society) is the other essential feature of a monorail system?

   A) Monorail systems are above ground level
   B) Monorail systems use cable propulsion
   C) Monorail vehicles are wider than the guideway that supports them
   D) Monorail vehicles have their own independent power source

Where is the engine of a maglev train located?

   A) It doesn't have an engine - magnetic attraction and repulsion make it run
   B) In the track
   C) In the guideway walls
   D) In the front car

080

G ermany and Japan are both developing maglev train technology. Which of these is NOT a difference between Germany's EMS system and Japan's rival EDS system?

A) The Japanese trains run on wheels at low speeds

B) The Japanese trains are designed to travel faster than the German trains

C) The Japanese trains levitate higher above the guideway than the German trains

D) The Japanese trains use supercooled, superconducting electromagnets

081

T o operate, roller coasters depend on Newton's First Law of Motion. What does this state?

A) What goes up must come down

B) He who pays the piper calls the tune

C) For every action there is an equal and opposite reaction

D) An object in motion tends to stay in motion

The Magic of Science

It is amazing what has been invented, developed and manufactured in our technological age. How much do you know of what's been going on in laboratories all over the world? Test your knowledge of the miracle of science with these questions.

Which of the following plants is NOT likely to be genetically modified to make eco-friendly fuels in the future?

    A) Soya bean
    B) Sugar beet
    C) Pineapple
    D) Rapeseed

What is cloning?

    A) A genetically very similar organism is created in a lab nonsexually
    B) A genetically identical organism is created nonsexually in a lab
    C) A new organism is produced by magic
    D) A genetically different organism, but with identical appearance, is created nonsexually in a lab

084

In what bizarre way have scientists been able to artificially manufacture silk?

A) They populated a former chicken farm with spiders

B) They discovered that silk can be extracted from human hair

C) They set up a silkworm factory on the Moon, where low gravity increases production rates

D) They genetically modified a goat by inserting a spider's genes. Silk proteins can be extracted from the goat's milk

085

How does light travel through a fiber-optic cable?

A) By magic

B) By reflection - it bounces off the lining of the cable

C) By conversion - it is converted into vibrations that travel along the fibers

D) By absorption - the fibers absorb and transmit the light

The Magic of Science

Which of the following is NOT a form of cloning?

A) Gardeners taking cuttings to grow new plants

B) A chemical stimulus being given to an unfertilized lizard's egg so it develops into an adult

C) The seed from a plant germinating

D) A mother giving birth to identical twins

What is the connection between Carbon 14 dating (used to date archeological artifacts) and outer space?

A) Life on Earth was created by aliens

B) Carbon 14 consists of particles of dust from asteroids

C) The formation of Carbon 14 is triggered by cosmic rays entering the Earth's atmosphere from outer space

D) Carbon 14 dating techniques were developed in order to find out the age of the Moon

The Magic of Science

088

What is a fiber-optic cable made from?

   A) Strands of copper wire, thinner than human hair
   B) Strands of very pure glass, about the diameter of a human hair
   C) Fluorescent gel in a rubber tube
   D) Real human hair

089

What does a refractor telescope use to collect light from a distant object and bring it to a focus?

   A) A glass lens
   B) A concave mirror
   C) A convex mirror
   D) A small imp with very powerful vision

090

What does the name LASER mean?

   A) Light And Sound Electronic Radiation
   B) Live Ace Super Evil Rocketbuster
   C) Light Amplification by Stimulated Emission of Radiation
   D) Linked Accelerated Source of Echo Radiation

The Magic of Science

Why might a scientist say that a sparkler is like candy?

A) It is brightly colored

B) It is given to children on holidays such as 4th July

C) It may contain sugar (to bind together the fuel and other compounds)

D) It contains a high level of latent energy

Why would an optometrist prescribe a minus lens for a patient's eyeglasses?

A) This lens is thinnest in the middle and moves the focal point backwards. It's used to correct myopia (nearsightedness)

B) This lens is shaped like a cylinder and corrects the distorted vision caused by the condition of astigmatism

C) This lens is thickest in the middle and moves the focal point forwards. It's used to correct hyperopia (farsightedness)

D) This lens will enable the patient to enjoy 3-D effects at the movies

The Magic of Science

093

How do you stop a seismograph machine from shaking while it is measuring the strength of an earthquake?

> **A)** Anchor it very securely to the ground
>
> **B)** Mount it on ball bearings
>
> **C)** Attach it to a very heavy weight, perhaps about 1,000 pounds
>
> **D)** Mount it on a levitating platform above the ground

094

The Richter Scale (the standard scale used to measure earthquakes) is described as a "logarithmic scale." What does this mean?

> **A)** As you go down the scale, each number describes a tremor half the size of the one before
>
> **B)** As you go up the scale, each number describes a tremor 10 times larger than the one before
>
> **C)** It is similar to a musical scale
>
> **D)** As you go up the scale, each number describes a tremor one unit greater than the one before

The Magic of Science

What is the eyepiece lens of a telescope used for?

A) It takes the light that has been focused by a lens or mirror, and magnifies it so you can view the image

B) It stops the imp inside the telescope from escaping

C) It brings the light from a distant object to a small focal point

D) It can be rotated to clarify a fuzzy image

How do scientists use DNA fingerprinting to compare samples from a suspect and a crime scene?

A) They search for sequences of Xs and Ys in the DNA

B) They look for patterns of colors along the strands of DNA

C) They count the number of repeating sequences in defined areas of the DNA

D) They look for an evil gene that indicates a criminal mind

097 What might be added to the black powder in a firecracker to make it flash more brightly?

- **A)** Charcoal
- **B)** Aluminum
- **C)** Colored paint powder
- **D)** Sulfur

---

098 What is the most important feature that determines the power of a telescope?

- **A)** The magnification power of the eyepiece lens
- **B)** The curvature of the primary mirror
- **C)** The aperture (the diameter of the lens or mirror)
- **D)** The eyeglasses worn by the imp

---

099 What is a nanobot?

- **A)** A microscopic robot, the size of a molecule, which could be injected into the human body to zap diseases
- **B)** A huge, powerful robot, designed to be used for tasks such as construction work and heavy lifting
- **C)** A robot for domestic use - it will do laundry, ironing, cleaning, and so on
- **D)** The grandmother of all robots

The future is now. All these questions will test you on how the machines of today enhance our lives and how our future might look. What do you really know about the rise of the machines?

How does a refrigerator use the liquid called the refrigerant to cool the air inside?

- **A)** It is condensed to absorb heat
- **B)** It is circulated rapidly to absorb heat
- **C)** It fills the walls of the refrigerator to insulate it
- **D)** It is evaporated to absorb heat

How does a fingerprint scanner read an image of your finger?

- **A)** It turns the surface of your finger into a capacitor plate which measures its electrical charge
- **B)** It measures the electric current generated by your skin
- **C)** It runs a beam of ultraviolet light across your finger
- **D)** It uses a laser beam to make a map of the surface of your finger

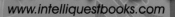

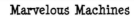
102

How are the Mars Exploration Rover (MER) robots powered?

A) They carry powerful, long-lasting batteries

B) They have turbines to capture the power of the Martian winds

C) They have gasoline engines

D) They generate power with solar panels and store it in their batteries

103

How does an MER robot use a RAT tool?

A) It's a device to detect any rodent life on Mars

B) It's a Rock Abrasion Tool - a drill used to bore samples of Martian rock

C) It's a Rover Acceleration Turbo - it gives the robot a boost in speed when needed

D) It's a Robotic Accuracy Tool - a method to double-check the data recorded by the robot before transmitting it to Earth

What system was devised by NASA to slow down the Mars Rover vehicle from its 12,000mph/19,320kph approach speed and protect it during landing?

A) A heat shield, a parachute, retro-rockets and airbags

B) A long elastic rope attached to a main spaceship in orbit above the planet

C) A parachute, retro-rockets and airbags

D) A heat shield, a parachute and airbags

How does a snow gun create artificial snowflakes?

A) A team of snow fairies inside the machine individually crafts the snowflakes

B) Water is frozen into blocks, then exploded with a small charge to create tiny fragments

C) A jet of water is fired through a freezer compartment

D) Cooled water is combined with compressed air, which atomizes it and blows it out of the machine

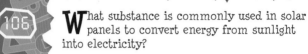

106 What substance is commonly used in solar panels to convert energy from sunlight into electricity?

- **A)** Carbon
- **B)** Steel
- **C)** PVC
- **D)** Silicon

107 What stops a robotic lawnmower from mowing the flowers?

- **A)** A wire is buried underground to guide it
- **B)** It is programmed to hate the scent of flowers
- **C)** It has an inbuilt radar system
- **D)** It has a sensor that can detect the edge of the lawn

108 What is the most common type of robot used in manufacturing?

- **A)** A jointed arm, designed to move in a similar way to a human arm
- **B)** A vacuum cleaner to clear up debris
- **C)** A humanoid model that brings refreshments to the factory workers
- **D)** A 5-fingered claw, similar to a human hand

How would a bumper sensor be used on a robot?

A) It would send a beam towards a target object, and guide the robot to it

B) When the robot bumps into an object, it is programmed to pull out a hammer and destroy it

C) When a robot bumps into an object, the sensor analyzes it and stores the data

D) When the robot bumps into an object, it is programmed to turn around and move away

---

What mechanism can be built into a robot that walks on legs, to stop it falling over?

A) Very large, flat feet

B) A balance system made from gyroscopes

C) A balance system made from a pendulum within a cradle

D) Extendible stabilizers

111 **H**ow do the MER robots "see" so they can navigate around?

A) A radar system

B) Three pairs of black-and-white cameras on the front, back and mast of the Rover

C) Two fully working models of the human eye, attached to the front of the Rover

D) An advanced color camera on a pivot system, on top of the Rover

112 **W**hat might you use a "puppet robot" for?

A) Connect it to another robot to download a program or learn a new task

B) Wear it on your hand, to carry out dirty or unpleasant tasks such as vehicle maintenance

C) Put on a performance to entertain young children

D) Send it to explore an inaccessible or dangerous place such as a volcano, using remote-control

Tackle your knowledge of those structures around you and what makes them fabulous feats of engineering by answering the following questions.

What is a smart structure?

A) A building totally made of steel
B) A type of scaffolding
C) A building that is being developed to withstand earthquakes
D) A building that reacts to light

How might blasters tackle a typical building implosion?

A) Explode the top stories first, followed by the middle, and finally the lower levels
B) Explode the major support columns on the lower floors first and then a few upper stories. Gravity does the rest
C) Explode charges all the way up the middle of the building in one go, so the sides fall inwards
D) Pack explosives in everywhere and blow up the whole lot in one go

115

What shape are the foundations of a skyscraper?

A) Inverted cone shaped - they get narrower as they go further into the ground

B) Pyramid shaped - they get wider as they go further into the ground

C) Cube shaped

D) Rectangular - they mirror the shape of the building above

116

What type of bridge would you most likely build to cross a short gap (say 100 feet/30 meters)?

A) A beam bridge (a rigid horizontal structure resting on two piers)

B) A suspension bridge (cables are strung across the gap, and the bridge is suspended from them)

C) An arch bridge (a semicircular structure with abutments on each end)

D) A rope bridge (two parallel ropes with planks fixed across them)

What is the purpose of the cables on a suspension bridge?

117

- **A)** They are for maintenance workers to climb to reach the towers
- **B)** They transfer the force of compression, which is pushing down on the roadway, to the supporting towers
- **C)** They are decorative
- **D)** They stop the bridge from swaying

Why are the roadways on bridges often made from several overlapping sections?

118

- **A)** The bridge is too long for a single section to be used
- **B)** It shows where the bridge has been patched up and repaired over the years
- **C)** To make the bridge more flexible under pressure (e.g. during earth tremors)
- **D)** To break up dangerous resonant vibrations which could travel through the bridge and cause structural damage

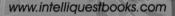

119 What stops a crane from toppling over when it is lifting a load?

A) The tires are deflated so the crane sits low on the ground

B) Steel cables are used to peg the crane to the ground, like the ropes on a tent

C) The crane has outriggers, like extendible legs, and a huge removable counterweight behind the cab

D) The truck is constructed with a solid lead plate in the base of the chassis

120 Which of these is NOT part of the safety system in an elevator?

A) Up to about eight extra steel cables in case one should snap

B) Electromagnetic brakes that clamp shut if the power fails

C) A "governor" braking system, which stops the cable if it runs too fast

D) Huge airbags at the foot of the shaft, which inflate if the car falls

What supports the weight of a skyscraper?

A) Rows of vertical steel columns

B) A grid of horizontal steel girders

C) The external walls

D) A massive steel pin in the center of the building

How much horsepower would the motor of a typical escalator be likely to have?

A) 100

B) 25

C) 1

D) 500

How does a hydraulic elevator work?

A) A fluid-driven piston mounted inside a cylinder pulls the car up from above

B) A fluid-driven piston mounted inside a cylinder pushes the car up from below

C) The cable that pulls up the elevator is attached to a hydraulic pump

D) Water is pumped into the elevator shaft to raise the car, and pumped out again to lower it

It's cool to be a computer whizz so exercise all that technological information you're storing and see how many of the following questions you can get right.

124

How does the image get from a webcam onto a computer?

A) The image is converted into HTML programming, so it can be displayed on a Web page

B) Software turns the image into a JPEG file and uploads it to your Web server - it can then be shown on a Web page

C) No conversion is required - the image is simply broadcast straight onto the Web

D) The image is broken down into its component colors, which are then converted into Javascript for Web display

125

Approximately how many chips are inside your computer's microprocessor?

A) None

B) 250

C) 1

D) 500,000

If you open a file on your computer, what part of the memory stores any changes until you save and close it?

126

A) Read Only Memory (ROM)

B) Random Access Memory (RAM)

C) The operating system

D) Nowhere - the changes are not stored

In computer-speak, what is a Trojan Horse?

127

A) A virus that will replicate itself rapidly, transmitting itself to other computers by using your e-mail address book

B) A computer program that appears innocent, such as a game, but contains malicious coding. If you run it, it may damage your computer files or allow a hacker access

C) A game program that allows you to re-create your own version of the famous siege of Troy

D) A piece of software that protects your computer from viruses and hackers

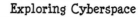

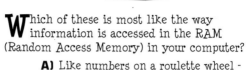

128

Which of these is most like the way information is accessed in the RAM (Random Access Memory) in your computer?

A) Like numbers on a roulette wheel - you can't predict what you will get

B) Like stops on a bus route - you have to go through them in sequence to reach the one you want

C) Like sweets on a counter - you can pick out whatever you want

D) Like balloons being released from a net - everything comes in one go

129

What does virtual memory do?

A) It exists to record the Web sites you have visited during an Internet session, so that you can call them up again

B) It helps you to remember your dreams

C) If there are areas that you rarely use in the RAM of your computer, it copies them to the hard drive to create more space

D) Nothing - it is memory that your computer theoretically has, but you can't actually use it

What is the relationship between bits and bytes?

A) There is no relationship between the two measurements

B) A byte is a large bit

C) A bit consists of 10 bytes

D) A byte consists of 8 bits

130

What does a SETI@home screensaver do?

A) When your computer is inactive, its power is used to process data from the Search for Extraterrestrial Intelligence - a project to search for radio signals from other civilizations in outer space

B) It stands for Search Engine Total Internet: when your computer is inactive, its power is used to search for interesting sites throughout the Internet

C) It's a power-saving device, previously only available to business users, which you can now use on your computer at home

D) It's a special offer on computer monitors bought over the Internet

131

132 **W**hat is an ALU?

A) The Affective Loop Unit within the RAM, which remembers common sequences of keystrokes

B) The term for an entire computer system - it's a contraction of the words All Units

C) The Arithmetic/Logic Unit within a microprocessor, which carries out mathematical calculations such as addition and subtraction

D) An Anterior Linked Unicode - a linking system between different levels of computer memory

133 **W**hat is HTML?

A) It's a strange, secret code used by computer experts when they don't want anyone else to understand them

B) It's a programming language used to create web pages

C) It's a secret military research establishment in the Nevada desert

D) It's a virus that infects your computer by changing parts of the programming, causing serious malfunctions

Why would you want to have a heuristic filter?

134

   A) It's a fine mesh screen that you place on your computer monitor to cut out glare

   B) It is a sophisticated spam filter that works by identifying word patterns and frequencies

   C) It's a piece of software that identifies Web pages with inappropriate content and blocks them

   D) It's a device which protects your computer from damage during power surges, by absorbing the electric current

How do computer viruses work?

135

   A) By sending electronic pulses through your computer to disrupt the mechanisms within it

   B) By copying themselves to locations on your hard drive and setting up files with innocent-looking names

   C) By embedding false data within the memory and wiping out your data

   D) By releasing tiny robotic bacteria inside the computer

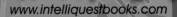

136

How might your computer turn into a zombie machine?

A) An evil magician places a spell on it, causing it to start up at the dead of night

B) A hacker breaks into your computer while you are working, and you lose control of the keyboard and mouse

C) It becomes infected by a virus that causes images from horror movies to appear on your screen

D) It becomes infected by a virus that allows spammers to access your computer and send e-mails from it

137

What does a Web spider do?

A) It's a piece of software that "crawls" around the World Wide Web, listing and indexing the words on every page it finds

B) It's a piece of programming that enables Web pages to be linked together in a network

C) It's a piece of software used by search engines to prevent some search results being displayed

D) It's a clever device that catches flies that land on your computer

What does a spambot do?

- **A)** It's a program that searches websites for the @ sign which denotes an e-mail address, so that the address can then be targeted by a spammer
- **B)** It's a program that you install on your computer to "bounce" spam e-mails, so it appears that your e-mail address is not valid
- **C)** It's a piece of software that enables spammers to send out batches of millions of e-mails at one time
- **D)** It's a type of robot which is sent to seek out spammers

138

How did the word "bit" come about, in relation to computers?

- **A)** It simply means a small piece, or bit, of data
- **B)** It is a contraction of the words "binary digit," because computers operate using the binary number system
- **C)** It stands for Big Itemized Tags, the markers that divide parcels of data
- **D)** It stands for Binary Indexed Text

139

140

A "Googlewhack" is what happens when you enter two unrelated words into the Internet search engine Google, and after scanning the content of over four billion Web pages...

A) It finds none that contain both words

B) It finds exactly one million pages containing both words

C) It generates an error message with a picture of a baseball player getting a painful injury

D) It finds only one that contains both words

141

What is Bluetooth?

A) A way to connect electronic devices without wires, using infrared radiation to communicate

B) A way to connect electronic devices without wires, using ultraviolet light to communicate

C) A way to connect electronic devices without wires, using radio waves to communicate

D) A condition affecting computer game enthusiasts who have been chewing gum whilst playing

What is WiFi?

A) Connecting separate computers using radio transmitter/receiver devices similar to walkie-talkies, but operating at a higher frequency

B) It connects separate electronic devices using ultraviolet radiation to communicate instead of wires

C) It stands for Wide Fidelity, a type of sound system similar to HiFi, but built into a computer

D) It means Windows Fidelity, and refers to the window which appears on your computer screen when you open a music file

What might a silicon chip contain?

A) Simply a sheet of pure, perfectly smooth silicon

B) Anything up to thousands of microscopic strands of copper, fused to the surface

C) Anything up to many millions of transistors etched onto the surface

D) Grains of fine sodium chloride

Cellphones and Networks

There used to be a time when letters used to be the quickest way to contact people over a long distance. Now you can call anyone from anywhere, from the middle of a field to the middle of a desert. Do you know how?

144

Why are cell phones so called?

A) They were invented by a convict in his prison cell

B) They all have a power cell (battery) inside them

C) The word "cell" stands for "call everyone loads line"

D) They cover large areas by dividing them into many small cells

145

How do polyphonic cell phones differ from standard (non-polyphonic) ones?

A) Polyphonic phones are much more expensive

B) Polyphonic phones have full Internet access

C) Polyphonic phones can play more than one musical note at a time

D) Polyphonic phones can transmit pictures as well as sound

Cellphones and Networks

A cell phone opens two different channels when you are making a call. Why is this?

A) One is for the call, the other is for back-up in case it fails

B) One is for the government, so that they can listen in on your call

C) One is for the cell you are in, the other is for the adjacent one

D) One is for each caller, so that they can speak and listen at the same time

How do cell phones transmit their signals?

A) Infrared radiation

B) Microwaves

C) Radio waves

D) Ultraviolet radiation

In a typical analog cell-phone system in the United States, about how many different frequencies does each cell-phone carrier receive to use across an average city?

A) 800

B) 400

C) 200

D) 100

149

$\mathbf{A}$nd what is the maximum number of people who can be talking on their phones at the same time in any one cell?

A) 32
B) 44
C) 56
D) 84

150

$\mathbf{I}$n an analog system, what is the typical size of each cell?

A) 5 square miles
B) 10 square miles
C) 20 square miles
D) 50 square miles

151

$\mathbf{W}$hen someone making a cell-phone call moves from one cell to another, their phone gets a signal on a control channel telling it to change to a new frequency pair used in the new cell. This is known as a:

A) Palm off
B) Hand off
C) Brush off
D) Push off

Cellphones and Networks

Why are digital cell-phone systems now preferred to analog?

- **A)** They are newer
- **B)** They are cooler
- **C)** They have lower overall power consumption
- **D)** You can fit more channels within a given bandwidth

A cell phone that will work on both analog and digital networks is called:

- **A)** Dual Band
- **B)** Dual Choice
- **C)** Dual Mode
- **D)** Dual Channel

GSM is now the international standard for digital cell phone systems. What does GSM stand for?

- **A)** Great System for Mobiles
- **B)** Global Speech and Messaging
- **C)** Global System for Mobile Communications
- **D)** Good Speech Mechanism

155 WAP (Wireless Application Protocol) and GPRS (General Packed Radio Service) are two methods cell-phone users can access the Internet. What is the most important difference between them?

A) GPRS is more reliable than WAP

B) GPRS works anywhere, while WAP only works in major population centers

C) GPRS is more expensive than WAP

D) GPRS is always on, while with WAP you have to dial up the service

156 Which of these statements about GSM cell phones is untrue?

A) They do not require a SIM card to operate

B) They include error-correction algorithms to reduce noise and improve message quality

C) They use encryption to make calls more secure

D) They use Time Division Multiple Access rather than Code Division Multiple Access

Can you believe there was a time before television? It can be a very powerful tool so investigate your depth of knowledge on this marvelous medium.

How many data-storage layers can a DVD have?

A) 1

B) 2 (1 on each side)

C) 4 (all on one side)

D) 4 (2 on each side)

How does a jumbo TV screen in a sports stadium work?

A) Around 100 cathode ray tubes are arranged in a grid and controlled by computer

B) It has a giant cathode ray tube, like a domestic TV but several meters long

C) Light emitting diode (LED) modules - collections of colored lights - are arranged in a grid and controlled by computer

D) The image is projected onto a screen from a projector on the opposite side of the stadium

159 **W**hat is the "plasma" in a plasma TV set?

A) A gel made from phosphorus, sandwiched between two glass plates

B) Hundreds of thousands of tiny cells, filled with neon or xenon gas

C) A layer of neon or xenon gas, trapped between two glass plates

D) A supernatural substance produced by ghosts

160 **W**hat colors are used in the pixels which make up a TV picture?

A) Red, orange, yellow, green, blue, indigo and violet

B) Red, yellow and blue

C) Black, white and ultraviolet

D) Red, green and blue

161 **H**ow does a DVD compare to a CD?

A) It holds about half the amount of data

B) It holds about 30 times the amount of data

C) It holds about 7 times the amount of data

D) It's the same thing

What happens when the image from a video camera is "rasterized" to turn it into a TV picture?

A) The colors are altered slightly, as a TV screen only has a limited range of color

B) The edges are trimmed so that the picture fits the shape of the TV screen

C) The film is speeded up slightly

D) The picture is turned into rows of individual dots (pixels)

What might cause "ghosting" (a double image) when you're watching a cable TV channel?

A) A fault in the wires of the coaxial cable, which carries the cable signal

B) Interference from the broadcast radio signal of the same channel, because it travels at a different speed from the cable signal

C) Interference from another TV channel

D) A poltergeist inside your TV set

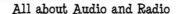

All about Audio and Radio

The radio may be on in the background or you may be playing music but when you're sitting listening to either do you know just what is going on to make that possible? Test yourself with the following questions on the amazing technological advancements of sound.

164 What does MP3 stand for?

A) Music Player 3

B) Music Compression Process 3

C) Moving Picture Experts Group Audio Layer-3

D) Maximum Listening Power 3

165 What does the MP3 system do to music recordings?

A) It enhances the quality of the sound

B) It removes noise and interference

C) It reduces the number of bytes dramatically, but without seriously affecting the quality of the recording

D) It reduces the number of bytes dramatically, by reducing the quality of the recording

All about Audio and Radio

What does monaural (mono) sound mean?

A) The music is flat, boring and toneless

B) Sound is recorded on several tracks or channels, but from microphones in one position

C) All the sound is recorded on one track or channel (e.g. a single groove in a vinyl record)

D) Sound is recorded on several tracks or channels, but played through only one speaker

How many minutes of music can a CD normally store?

A) 65

B) 74

C) 92

D) It depends what type of music it is

Which of these uses radio waves to operate?

A) Cordless phone

B) GPS receiver

C) Microwave oven

D) All of the above

How does a CD player read the information on a CD?

- **A)** A tiny stylus (needle) runs along the track on the CD
- **B)** A laser beam is projected into the CD track. When it meets a pit it is absorbed, and when it meets a lump it bounces a pulse back into the projector
- **C)** A laser beam is bounced off the lumps and pits on the CD track and onto an optical pick-up, which detects the changes in reflectivity
- **D)** An infrared beam is bounced off the lumps and pits on the CD track, generating a pattern of hot and cool spots

Speakers have different drivers (electromagnets attached to flexible cones) to produce different sound frequencies. Which is the largest?

- **A)** The tweeter
- **B)** The woofer
- **C)** The midrange speaker
- **D)** Could be any of these

Approximately how many bytes does the average (three minute long) track on a CD occupy?

A) 32,000,000

B) 650,000

C) 48,000

D) 500

What is the usual form of stereophonic (stereo) sound we listen to on domestic audio systems?

A) Numerous microphones in different positions are used to record sound on many channels

B) Two microphones in different positions are used to record sound on a number of channels

C) The sound is recorded through a single microphone, which can distinguish whether it comes from the left or right, and recorded on two channels

D) Two microphones in different positions are used to record sound on two channels

Are you crazy about cars or are they just something that take you back and forth and annoy you when they break down. So much goes into making these transport marvels so keep your motor running, get those engines firing on all cylinders and see if you can race through the questions.

173

How would you measure the "horsepower" of a car?

A) Connect the back bumper to a team of horses, accelerate the car forwards, and see how many horses it takes before the car goes backwards

B) Measure the time and distance it takes for the car to accelerate from 0-60mph

C) Connect the engine to a dynamometer, which places a load on the engine and measures the amount of power that it produces against the load

D) Place a fixed metal bar fitted with pressure pads across the front of the car, floor the accelerator, and measure the pressure generated

174

What did Bugatti use to create a 1,000-horsepower engine for their amazing Veyron car?

A) Four separate turbochargers and a 16-cylinder engine

B) Rocket-boosters

C) A transmission system with eight gears and a highly responsive clutch pedal

D) The engine is extremely large but constructed from lightweight materials

175

Why do Ferrari cars feature the emblem of a prancing black horse?

A) The symbol is a reference to the impressive horsepower of Ferrari engines

B) The symbol was painted on the airplane of an ace WW1 Italian fighter pilot, and Enzo Ferrari knew his parents

C) The high octane fuel used in the early Ferrari cars was named Cavalla Nera (Black Horse)

D) Enzo Ferrari kept a stable of horses, and his favorite was a black stallion

176 What is meant by the term "hybrid car?"

A) A car that uses liquefied petroleum gas (LPG) fuel

B) A car that can be converted to travel through water like a boat

C) A car that can switch between four-wheel drive and two-wheel drive

D) A car that is powered by both a gasoline tank and an electric motor

177 Which of the following are NOT caused by underinflating a car's tires?

A) The tires wear more on the outside than the inside

B) The car uses more fuel than it should

C) Acceleration is slower than it should be

D) Heat builds up in the tires

178 Which of these substances would NOT be used to make a tire?

A) Steel cables

B) Cotton cords

C) Polyester fabric

D) Rubber

What is the role of a camshaft in a car's engine?

179

A) It makes the attractive growl associated with performance cars

B) It generates the sparks to ignite the gasoline

C) It pushes the gasoline into the combustion chamber

D) It rotates to open and close the intake and exhaust valves

How does pressure on the brake pedal cause a car to stop?

180

A) A lever engages with the wheel axle, and the friction slows the wheels

B) The movement is transmitted to the wheels through hydraulics: a piston pushes non-compressible liquid through a system of cylinders and pipes

C) A piston squirts brake fluid into expandable chambers next to the wheels, resulting in pressure against them

D) Air is pumped vigorously forwards, counteracting the motion of the car

181 What fills an air bag in a car when it inflates?

- **A)** A cylinder of compressed air underneath the chassis is released
- **B)** A powerful pump draws air into the bag from outside the car
- **C)** Sodium azide and potassium nitrate react to form nitrogen gas
- **D)** The crash impact causes separate cylinders of hydrogen and oxygen to break, combine and expand

182 Why do some tires have deep channels in the same direction as the tread?

- **A)** To give extra traction in soft mud or snow
- **B)** To make them look larger and more impressive
- **C)** To help prevent hydroplaning (losing contact with the road surface when driving through standing water)
- **D)** To help prevent sideways skids in icy conditions

As mementoes of friends, family and vacations photographs are brilliant but what goes into creating those images, that fill us with so much joy, is at your fingertips. Discover how much you know in the following questions.

How is light from the subject focused in a digital camera?

A) No focus is needed - the light falls directly onto photocells that record it

B) A series of lenses focuses light onto a semiconductor device that records it electronically

C) The light goes straight into the camera's computer, which focuses it

D) A series of mirrors directs the light onto a digital film

What substance is used in the coating on a photographic film, to react to the light?

A) Silver halide crystals

B) Copper sulfate crystals

C) Melanin

D) Gelatin

185 Why is lying on a beach like taking a photograph?

- **A)** The sea reflects the sunlight as brightly as a camera flash bulb
- **B)** They are both things you do on vacation
- **C)** The process of photochemistry takes place when your skin develops a suntan. Photochemistry also records an image on a film
- **D)** The substances in sun lotion are similar to those in photographic film

186 What is the particular characteristic of "fast" film?

- **A)** It's perfect to use with a fast shutter speed, for example in very bright conditions
- **B)** It's very smooth, so it spools very quickly through the camera
- **C)** It's very sensitive to light, so it can be used in dimly lit conditions
- **D)** It doesn't last very long

Fabulous Photography

What sort of pictures would you take if you chose a lens with a low focal length for your camera?

- **A)** They would show a wide view of the whole subject, but at low magnification
- **B)** They would be slightly blurred
- **C)** They would show a narrow view of part of the subject, at high magnification
- **D)** The horizon would always look slightly sloping

What is the modern equivalent of the clapperboard used in motion pictures?

- **A)** The sound and pictures are recorded together, so no clapperboard is needed
- **B)** A radio signal from the tape recorder transmits a time code directly onto the film
- **C)** A digital slate displays a time code from the tape recorder
- **D)** An electric shock is delivered to the cameraman to wake him up

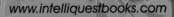

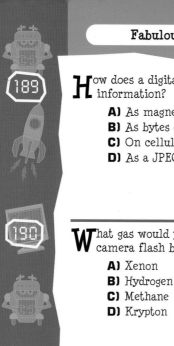

Fabulous Photography

189

How does a digital camcorder record visual information?

- **A)** As magnetic patterns
- **B)** As bytes of data
- **C)** On celluloid film
- **D)** As a JPEG file

190

What gas would you typically find inside a camera flash bulb?

- **A)** Xenon
- **B)** Hydrogen
- **C)** Methane
- **D)** Krypton

191

How is photographic film like Jell-O?

- **A)** It's edible
- **B)** It's semi-translucent
- **C)** It contains gelatin
- **D)** It changes its chemical composition in the presence of light

Fabulous Photography

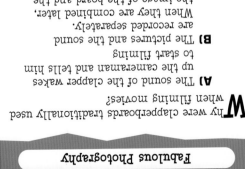

Why were clapperboards traditionally used when filming movies?

A) The sound of the clapper wakes up the cameraman and tells him to start filming

B) The pictures and the sound are recorded separately. When they are combined later, the image of the board and the sound of the clapper can be synchronized

C) The board is held at the same distance from the camera every time, so the focus can be checked before filming starts

D) The names of the actors and characters are recorded in case the director forgets

---

When you focus an SLR (Single lens Reflex) camera, what are you doing to the lens?

A) Changing its shape

B) Changing its angle

C) Moving it nearer or further from the film

D) Changing its size